The Things I Didn't Know to Wish For

The Things I Didn't Know to Wish For

by

Linda Hillringhouse

NQY Books™

The New York Quarterly Foundation, Inc.
Beacon, New York

NYQ Books™ is an imprint of The New York Quarterly Foundation, Inc.

The New York Quarterly Foundation, Inc.
P. O. Box 470
Beacon, NY 12508

www.nyq.org

First Edition

Set in New Baskerville

Layout and Overall Design by Raymond P. Hammond

Cover Art: *Sleepwalker in Town with Green Moon* by Linda Hillringhouse

Author Photograph by Mark Hillringhouse

Library of Congress Control Number: 2020933035

ISBN: 978-1-63045-069-4

For Mark

and in memory of my mother, father, and brother

Contents

Acknowledgements

I cannot possibly express the gratitude I feel for Gerald Stern and Maria Mazziotti Gillan for their great generosity in reading and commenting on my manuscript.

I am grateful to the following people who so kindly gave of their time and talent to help me, in one way or another, with the completion of this book: Dr. Irwin Badin, whose quality of listening led me to my own voice; Wendy Barnes, Bob Carnevale, Cat Doty, and Mark Hillringhouse for all the magical hours talking poetry around a table; Kristina Branch, for her belief in my work and for the editorial talent she selflessly provided throughout every stage of this book; Laura Boss, who always welcomed me back to poetry, no matter how long I'd been gone; Douglas Mackay for reading an early version of this book and for his steadfast support; Janice Peters for her astute reading of my work and for her abiding faith in it; Lynne Turner and Brie Turner O'Banion, who listened to various versions of some of these poems and offered candid, insightful responses. And, finally, I am deeply thankful to Raymond Hammond, publisher of NYQ Books, who brought this book into being.

I wish to gratefully acknowledge the editors of the publications in which some of these poems, or versions of them, originally appeared:

Lips: Prognostication; The Catalan Moon; The Sixties

New Ohio Review: Serenity Room; Calculations

Nimrod International Journal of Prose and Poetry: Lunch Money; Outside the Human Circle; Black Rattle; Ancient Peoples

Oberon: With No Thought of Skull

Paterson Literary Review: Something Luminous; The Bristol Plaza Hotel, Wildwood; At the Shore: End of August; Serenity Room: Doris; Revision; The Armenian Home; The Pool;

Virgin Sacrifice; Carline Drive; Fata Morgana; New Dress; Split Level; Walt Whitman at Willowbrook Mall

Prairie Schooner: Witness

RALPH (The Review of Arts, Literature, Philosophy and the Humanities): The Philosopher; Theory of Soul Mates; Mt. Carmel Retreat

Sequestrum: Amor Fati; At the Barcelona Zoo; Son of Sam

Shrew Literary Magazine: Semblance; Breakdown in Retrospect; Tatiana; Template

The Great Falls: An Anthology of Poems about Paterson, New Jersey: The Essex Mill, Paterson

Lunch Money, Outside The Human Circle, and Black Rattle received the *Pablo Neruda Prize for Poetry* from *Nimrod International Journal*, judged by Philip Levine.

The Bristol Plaza Hotel, Wildwood received the *Allen Ginsberg Poetry Award* from *The Paterson Literary Review*.

New Dress

I'm going to tell you something even I don't know
& I don't know how I'll find it but I'm going somewhere,
down into something, looking for that thing that I will finally
tell you & a girl appears walking her way back to the living
room in which she will wait for her parents to come back
from their first trip. She's wearing the dress, the heart-stopping,
paralyzingly beautiful dress that Lenore, the neighbor, has bought her—
red plaid, big crinoline & best of all, suspended from the belt, a real plastic
pocket watch forever displaying seven o'clock. She is aglow, for when they
behold her, they will run to her, kiss her, lift her aloft & she will see herself
in their eyes & grow into someone alive in the miracle of the world who will
take root joyously and in sorrow.

She stands, arms outstretched like a supplicant or little model & they are walking
through the door & her father picks her up but unbelievably her mother walks by,
smiling, in the full beauty of her days, at the neighbor & past the dress like no other
& the thing that was known & not known became flesh & I'm finally telling you that
right there in Lenore's living room time stopped & the future turned to dust.

Template

I lay there, head back to stanch the nosebleed, washcloth
over my face like a savage veil, princess pajamas pulled down,
the drafty room, the disembodied hand landing like a spider.

That was me in your care that day. Was it my mother's apathy
that gave you courage—or my separation from the flock?
Or was it just you, your father's gift from God, getting his due?

When I called him forty years later, I was standing in the hall
of my parents' condo in Florida facing a studio shot of me
and my brother in playsuits sitting on a log in the middle
of a sunny cardboard farm.

He said he was just a kid but I told him he had a car. I didn't
mention the night he parked in front of a closed candy store
under a streetlight, didn't tell him how I noticed the shadows
of leaves trembling on the dashboard

as he tried to teach me how to handle that insistent creature
in his lap and I didn't say that he gave me another lesson
in his mother's closet, the family a room away, while he pretended
to look for a tie, my face swept by shirttails.

These events stand alone, and since they are mine to keep, I want
to say something without forgiveness or mercy, but with bitterness
lodged in the tongue like a weed: There were others who used me
but you were the first—and I saw your reckless skull behind every
boy's face and, later, behind every man's.

The Pool

For the Montclair girls, Maureen, Barbara, and Linda
and for the Clifton girls, Cheryl and Jackie

I would walk the sparkling asphalt road
past the reservoir and dull split levels
to meet my friends at Mary's, the tiny
corner gas station and convenience store
stocked with everything we needed: Twinkies,
Wonderbread, bologna, Yoohoo, the chocolate
drink with no chocolate in it—and we'd sit out back,
under the only old trees left in the neighborhood,
to eat our toxic lunches and laugh about some dare
I had just taken, using a made-up language on Mary
or making a cross-eyed drool face at her son who
pumped gas out front.

Then we'd cross the street and parade through the lobby
of the *Montclair Beach Club* like Lolita's-in-Training
and head up to the deck away from our canasta-crazed mothers
to read passages from *Marjorie Morningstar* or to savage some
"stuck up" girl whose only crime was dating a lifeguard.
We held forth on breasts: who had them, who didn't, how mine grew
while staying with my Aunt Lee in Sheepshead Bay and how a trip
to Brooklyn could be finessed. We worked our tans with giant reflectors,
holding them in front of our faces like holy books as we broke down the news:
who got caught smoking, got a hickey or horrible haircut, who had cramps,
who was doing it and how you could tell from the way they walked.

Sometimes we'd troop down from the deck to the pool and pray
for the courage and greatness to jump off the high dive and survive
the silent near death trip to the surface, to burst through the water
in triumph, to feel the worshipful eyes of the world upon us and stand
dripping on the cerulean cement, faces flawless in the sun, removing
our nose clips and ear plugs with the aplomb of Olympians and inspect
ourselves for a stray pubic hair or a partially exposed nipple, either of which
would mean death by embarrassment.

Then we'd strut over to the snack bar in our bathing suits to look for boys, order cokes and fries, and dance under the blue awning to the fabulous girl groups who taught us what to long for. When the sun began to go down, our mothers called to us to go get changed.

My mother and I would drive home silently. I dissolved into her disinterest until the next day when I walked down to Mary's to meet my friends under the trees and I reentered my body as they waved and shouted out my name.

Lunch Money

My mother sat naked
at the foot of the bed
bending over a golf sock
while my father
behind her back
peeked out from the blankets
contorting his face
in histrionic horror
at the gelatinous ass
and at, I presumed,
the parts of her
I could see from the front
to make the point
that surely he did not,
how could he,
are you kidding me,
never would he
ride this gray mare
to market

or was it to make the point
that I, living monument
to tits and ass,
was his first choice
were it not for a twist of fate
tying him forever
to this fleshy freak

or was it shame
that I knew
what this guy
high school hoops star
girl-slayer
and my savior
was forced to do
every night
after Johnny Carson

or maybe he was Oedipus
gears fatefully engaged
driving in reverse
straight back to his birth.

I bring him his pants,
the buckle heavy
in my hand,
he gives me
my lunch money
and I run to the corner
to catch the bus
that will take me
on the forty year ride
to the school
that teaches
one lesson only:
blood will beat out
knowledge every time.

The Curse

My sleepover friend Maureen
was in the mirror practicing smiles.
I was on the john staring at the tiny
Amish couples in weird hats standing
under the willows on the wallpaper
when I spotted a streak of blood across
my inner thigh, a dark message from
the manufacturer. I made Maureen swear
to keep her trap shut, especially to my mother,
who might drug me some night and dump me
in another state. She already had it in for me
since I wore the bikini and she went on a diet.

When she found the underpants behind the dresser,
she called my father at work despite my pleading
and told him to bring home a box of Kotex using
that fake dramatic voice I hated while I sat on the stairs
crying, an imaginary gun in my hand.

I'd coldcock her, get bus money and make it downtown
before he got home. I'd walk to the outskirts, through
the rickety neighborhoods and weedy cement lots,
to the river, to sink into the mud with the other animals
who were assigned their turf out of spite or neglect.

After School

One day I get home from school
and my mother's sitting in the kitchen
on the phone as usual, the clump of curly
black cord in her lap. She glances up at me,
but I can tell I haven't made it from her eye
to her brain and to prove this to my friends who
watch from the doorway, I grab the can of Yuban
off the counter and stand behind her and begin
to slowly spoon the coffee onto her head as my friends,
eyes popping, pyramid for a better view but nothing, just a toss
of the hair, so I say Mom, I did it with a goat in the Girls' Room today.
She smiles and nods, and my friends crack up—I am so ballsy and cool
and broken.

Split Level

The kitchen drawers, full of promise, yielded
only batteries, pencil stubs, pennies

In the cellar, the washer and dryer churned
like old world relatives fussing and sacrificing

In the bedroom, a satin lingerie envelope
held one pair of pantyhose, like a shriveled shadow

She had her thoughts and her husband had his, the slights
that destroyed daily the man he had planned to be

He would watch the game, the TV flickering like lives trying
to begin—and he would mow the lawn when lawn meant clover,
wild onion, not stones memorializing the unsaid

She would drive to the canasta game or the beauty parlor
and in her pocketbooks I looked for change and there
in the silken depths was a chaos of cast-aside things

We lived on a planet where language was in its infancy—
one thing became another and it was a mystery the way the past
grew bigger and bigger, sun streaming through the kitchen window,
warming the maple table as if this were a story and not my life.

Lockwood Drive

His bunk bed was rigged with blankets and toy guns
to look like a frontier fort. I sat at the edge of the lower bunk,
white cotton underpants pulled down, cowgirl skirt hiked up,
while he examined me with a bobby pin, not rushing or furtive
but as a frontier doctor, pushing aside the labia majora
with excruciating care as if expecting to find moving parts
or a prize and seemed disappointed at first, just there on his knees,
in his Davy Crockett hat, peering at the rubbery pink terrain until
he must have figured he was staring at a passageway and began tapping
around with the bobby pin but soon abandoned the exam in favor
of playing outside which was fine by me because I wanted to get back
to his parents' bedroom, to the bottle of Jergen's Lotion on the dressing table
to pump this marvel of invention which hit my hand like a secret welcome
to this land of adventure just around the corner.

Prognostication

It's not like I didn't get a heads up.
A warning was served in my sleep
on the backseat of a mini-bus
where I'm an old woman trying
to pull in enough oxygen to scream
as the knowledge that I'm about to die
mushrooms in my torso like a time lapse
tumor and there's no way out of the fact
that I had irrevocably and forever
blown it, wandered through my life
like a visitor and I jolt awake, heart
pounding, and it's still summer,
the blue Chevy in the driveway,
the four radio towers visible
from my bedroom window,
and strewn on my dresser, pink rollers,
mascara, a stuffed penguin from Seaside
Heights and one long cigarette butt hidden
in my sock drawer. My mother yells up
to me to go to *Food Fair* for cocktail onions,
my father's paying bills, my brother's practicing
the trombone for half-time at Clifton Stadium,
the phone and doorbell are ringing, and I have a date
with Ted Dybiak, captain of the football team.
I'm still a virgin and even with the early warning,
I am going to give myself away for a closet full
of cardboard crowns.

The Sixties

I wasn't present in the sixties
though Cam Ne was burning
deep in the TV and I looked
like Cher and wore a headband,
my political manifesto.

I was at Goddard College
majoring in hedonism,
which cost my father,
an appliance salesman,
$4000 a year, a fortune then,
when Kennedy and King were killed
and Shirley, the first black girl I knew,
got political and stopped talking to me.

Nicole, the first rich girl I knew,
drove a Porsche and lived in Scarsdale,
and one day, in protest of something,
threw down her lunch tray at the feet
of the college president, an action, which,
to me, was suicidal — having been bred
to fear the hand that fed me.

And the first gay guy I knew, Hector,
tripped his way through freshman year,
laughing at the silver flowers sprouting
in the clouds and at the hills that were
actually the backs of big kind creatures.
He was into the politics of amazement
and didn't care who you were —
I was a planet-mate, holy, beloved,
not a fucked-up girl from Jersey.

Beth, the first blind person I knew,
wore a brown poncho with red reindeers on it
and had the eyes of a prophet which filled me
with dread. I was surprised at how many
friends she had. I didn't understand how
they could bear not being seen.

The first guy I knew who died in Vietnam
was my friend Lynne's boyfriend, who was killed
on the Buddha's Birthday in Quang Ngai during
a truce. I looked for his name on the wall but saw
my own clueless face gazing out of the black granite
at the desecrated clouds.

I hear mechanical barks in the distance as if the dog
is only half invested, a rare thing for creatures
that don't reflect, and I'm thinking it's something
the way the past overtakes the present, the way the light
in the gingko tree across the street trembles as the sun
goes down and this light, it seems to me, someone who
never saw war, stupidly worth fighting for.

A man is yelling at the dog to shut up and why this is
worth noting I don't know and it's weird the way
insight finally arrives, but way too late
to do anyone any good.

Question

When Joanne & I made the cream cheese
caviar pie & filet mignon & lobsters
bathing in garlic butter, mounds of mashed
potatoes, coleslaw & a token salad
& ate it all with buttons & bras undone,
zippers down, Velvet Underground pounding,
cigarette breaks, weed, wine & finally the bust-out
blackout cake & peanut butter cup chasers,
were we gluttonous or just empty?

Tommy

My bedroom faced the neighbors
with the brilliant broken son
pulled out of Catholic school.
At twelve, Thorazine turned
his teeth green. He was nicer
than anyone was born to be,
gliding weightless, holding
a pencil out in front
like a baton, as if he were
conducting a telepathic chorus.
In his other hand, he held
a manila envelope, stuffed
with stories-in-progress.
I read one once, surprised
it wasn't good. I had assumed
he'd be compensated by whatever
it was that stood around and let
his life get wrecked.

Virgin Sacrifice

The first time I went to a gynecologist I was 18.
My parents knew him socially, and I ended up
on his examining table

in a room that looked like some kind of warped kitchen
with glass canisters on the counter containing disposable needles,
sterile pads, swabs, and instruments I prayed

he wouldn't be reaching for anytime soon. I lay there freezing
in knee socks and a thin cotton gown that opened in the front,
the ties a mere formality, my feet in stirrups as if

I were riding a horse in some capsized universe.
He puts on the gloves as I tell him, face burning,
that I have a "bump down there," but thinking

Who are you kidding, that's no bump, it's a lump, you'll be going
to chemo not college. His eyes are inches from my crotch and something
that feels like a butterfly corkscrew is opening its steel wings inside me

and I'm picturing him down there squinting, trying not to breathe, but then
he sits up, looks at me, and says Okay, bad news, it's cancer. I see the numbers
on the big round clock going squiggly and Time unhinging its jaw

to claim its prize, and in deadly earnest, I ask how long I've got and everything
getting smaller, and he laughs like I'm some kind of comedic genius and says
Oh, c'mon, I'm only kidding and I'm already so well-schooled in the art
of acquiescence that I apologize for not getting the joke.

Carline Drive

I'd walk home from the pool under a chlorine sky
back to the house on Carline Drive where talk
was for company, where I smoked in the shower
and imagined marathon make-outs to the sound
of the Marvelettes to drown out the stillness
of the split level, got dressed to the very edge
of whoredom, teased my hair into a hive, despite
rumors of skull-boring maggots, put on eyeliner
with the precision of a surgeon, snuck a blouse out
of my mother's closet, and finally heard my friends
blast the horn through the screens and I'd come flying
down the front steps into the drunken open arms
of that summer night with my name scrawled across the sky
and we'd peel back down the driveway, radio blasting
and by the time we turned the corner, the world was made
whole again.

Hedge Trimmers

How lost we were looking for something to shake the baby teeth out
of our blood.

The faux colonial table was strewn with bills, circulars, stamps,
bisected by the shadow of someone searching for more.

Souvenir spoons scooped out the souls of great American cities.

Cleansers, batteries, deodorizers leached into our sleep and burned
away segments of dreams. Lifetimes were wasted providing these things.

Hedge trimmers tamed the stubborn earth. Cicadas suggested
a power that would someday subdue us. Japanese beetles
skeletonized the maples.

Words fell between cushions. Seasons changed. Four red-eyed radio
towers ruined the sky.

The sun tried to offer us a big benevolent thing to move across
our minds, but nothing could save us and no one even knew
we needed saving.

A Hundred Sundays

In memory of my brother, Louis

No one had a name for it,
the chronic crying, the hitting,
so they sent him away
to a "child treatment center"
at the Jersey shore: *Brisbane.*
He was seven. I was five.

The main building had chicken wire over
the tall windows, walls painted unrefracted
green, a wrecked doll with horror movie hair
hanging from a wicker carriage, glass eyes
staring at the floor. He lived in a "cottage"
somewhere around the back and "Uncle Jim,"
who wore overalls, looked after him and the other
"cottage boys."

We'd drive down to Brisbane
every other Sunday for four years,
no matter the weather.
Once, on our way home,
we got stuck in a snowstorm
on the Garden State and Uncle Mike,
King of the Parkway, drove south
in the north lane to rescue us.

A hundred Sundays in the back seat
of the humped-up maroon and gray Dodge
with the brushed gray carpet that went
floor to ceiling. I would clutch my doll
to keep the sky from slipping into the car.

My brother wore a little man trench coat
with a belt and fur collar, his face bereft,
thorazined. He just wanted to go home,
be in his room, line up his baseball cards

29

on the maple desk; and see the same wallpaper
everyday, hear the same voices, bike bells, dog barks,
and I'd be there, sitting next to him on the floor,
watching Lassie.

Where did we go in winter? Were the arcades open?
In the summer we played skee ball on the boardwalk
or pedaled the swan boats joylessly in the man-made lake.
The grownups played Fascination, the hiss of the second
syllable always making me queasy.
What sin would send me away?

When he came home for good, he was eleven.
He begged me never to say Brisbane, to say
he'd been away at military school. He looked like
a teen idol but never had a girlfriend. He didn't understand
how it worked, didn't know words had a secret life beyond
the literal. He married the first girl who danced with him
at Joey's Pub. She was pretty but unkind.

He became an insurance agent, one of the best in the country.
He didn't know how to lie and customers knew it. Ten years
of big sales, travel, speeches, his only lucky run. But then
he got promoted and put a salesman in the hospital
because he couldn't read his eyes.

I avoided him, couldn't figure him out, the seclusion,
the monologues, the lashing out, the TV shows
from the fifties. And, besides, I was drowning
in my own life. When he called me, his message
was always the same: *Linda, pick up the phone.*
This is your brother. He'd say it three times.
I would roll my eyes.

One day he began to limp. When he called me at work,
I had never heard of multiple myeloma. I looked it up
and saw two years median survival. My parents and I
did not speak at full volume for three months. His wife
warned him not to expect a penny from her for treatment
and his teenage son teased him about his funeral.

When he stayed with us after the stem cell transplant,
my husband got him a green fleece jacket, just like his,
from L.L. Bean. He rarely took it off, and when
his head got shaved, he wore his beloved Yankees cap,
the only thing I kept.

And when my husband watched him measure water
to the rim of the glass and double check it, he guessed
he was autistic. Asperger's Syndrome. I stupidly thought
the diagnosis would offer comfort, that all the social blunders
and agonies he suffered would be redressed, but he didn't
want to know. It was just another failure.

I understand now why he loved the black and white world
inside the television when he was a boy. Nothing to decode.
No one to shame him. He could turn the world off when
it overwhelmed.

Louis, you were an innocent, kind and unprotected, uncomfortable
every minute of your life, and, for this, there is something in the world
I will never forgive.

Tatiana

I am twenty-five again
and I am not
in bed with
whoever you are.
I am not sleeping
until noon or wearing
my nightgown inside out.
I am not trying to sound smart
or make someone like me. Nor am I
getting stoned and painting happy
dead people with no eyes.
I am not telling some guy
I just met on campus
that my name is Tatiana
to sound exotic, to annihilate
the nobody in me.

Breakdown in Retrospect

For Lorraine
    Washington Square Clinic

Who was it that squeezed the green out of the leaves,
lived in negative space, hating half the alphabet
and all of antiquity? When I laughed, she sizzled like
a bad wire. When I cried, she levitated. At dawn, she
injected me with night.

I was twenty-eight when she rang my bell and handed me
two scans of the sky directly above my birth. One showed
a mass of spite protruding from a cloud, another showed
a baby, no longer viable, turned to stone. This is where
the first life ends and the second begins. The corrective one.
The one of sorrow.

Lorraine, we took her down back in the day, the dead weight,
the anomalous eye. Look at her now, the mud curls, the sludge
peeking from her pores. She's a big napper, takes sunlight
from a dropper, nibbles nuts from a thimble, stores her darkness
in a toe.

How could we have known she had already nailed her milky mirrors
to every door I would ever try to open?

Afterimage

That red-toothed thing that lies ruined on its rubber mattress
used to suck the rain out of the clouds. It loved to listen
to the sea creep towards the city. For fun, it would scare
farm animals. Once it ripped open the sky to reveal the winking
blue mouth of the universe. I couldn't sleep or eat. I couldn't
wake up or stop eating. And selves I would never meet
moved silently like caterpillars in their tents. It was like living
in a land where you don't speak the language, and your gestures
are inadvertently lewd, where troops of cousins, in cousinly love,
stroll arm in arm after dinner, but there you are, on the wrong street,
looking for your hotel. I was the moon hating borrowed light, longing
for the things of earth. And I longed to exist, not as an afterimage
but as a being finally released from a story in which I am my own
relentless antagonist.

St. Raphael

The night of the flamenco dancer,
her every move a flash of the double helix,
I saw fiery roses erupt on your arms.
At the hotel, in our calamitous bed,
a corpse sprung up between us
and we took it to Barcelona,
to the Church of the Holy Family
where it buried a tooth—
to Park Güell to see the mosaics
where it fractured the tiles
with its voltaic eyes—
and erased the prayers to the Virgin
with the acid of its thoughts.
In Cordoba, the Moorish stripes
of the Mezquita were the color
of baked blood. Raphael, Patron Saint
of the Blind, stood like a jumper
on the Roman Bridge. And in Seville,
the awnings drew back like prehistoric wings,
orange trees cast off their fruit and in the streets
couples crossed themselves when we walked by.

At the Barcelona Zoo

I stood alone in front of Snowflake,
the albino gorilla: behind bars
as if he'd committed some genetic crime,
a bouquet of fists for a face—
and hands that could've held
a can of beer or a breast

and a current, both holy and obscene,
passed between us, as if we
had inadvertently witnessed
God blowing life into the nostrils
of some probationary creature—
then walking away.

Outside the Human Circle

snails are dangerous,
gondolas and sponges,
designed by invalids
dreaming in solariums,
a kiss, the pact between
two lunatics.

Time is different here,
she drags around
a bag of bad weather
walking backwards.

The moon has sucked the dark
out of the night
and the rivers have reversed,
returning to their source
sick with mud and vertigo.

I am the ill-starred relative
who shines up your luck.
I am your sour mop,
your wart,
the catastrophe
that saves your crops.

You with bones
who boast shadows:
what quirk of the cosmos,
what curse across the crib
forbids me baptism,
makes me half-mammal
half-stone;
what dance of atoms,
ritual of ash,
will land me on your shore?

The Catalan Moon

You began to dismantle
the sad town we had built
but in the last stage
of demolition
I sold you on a trip to Spain
thinking I could
work some magic
on foreign soil,
telling my boss
the punishing lie
I needed time off
for my honeymoon
but there was no
tender reconciliation
in Barcelona,
just a bladder infection.

Really, what was I thinking,
that the Catalan moon
would wash our sheets in gold
and cauterize my soul,
that I would emerge from our room
like the Virgin of Montserrat
and the story of my transgressions
would play out on the stage
of your compassion?

What was I thinking,
a demon's tongue around
my neck, that you would
tackle me to safety
as shafts of light burst
through the clouds
like vast trade routes
to and from heaven
and the great saints

would stagger out of churches
and the sun would go black
and we'd land on your lawn
in summer, a second chance to see
the hydrangea in green shadow
and through some act of grace
I would be able to love you
with clarity and depth, as if
I had once been loved that way.

Semblance

The inamorata you concocted
running through the fields
of Watermill, Bach floating
from her ears, she's in a schmatta
from Marshall's, not a bodice
of rosebuds and birds

the angel you assembled,
lipstick the color of yes, crucifix
between her breasts, she washes
with Cetaphil and wears socks to bed

which is not to say we had nothing—
I miss the warm Guinness,
the bedroom carpet, a continent
of moonlight where we lay listening
to The Cantos, Pound's voice, raspy
and nasal and, to us, hilarious—
at dawn, green crept through the grass

and never did a man pursue a woman
he didn't want with such passion
that stones moved when he spoke.

At the VW Dealership

In the next cubicle, the wife does not speak.
Let he who is the purveyor of all things manly
take the wheel.

We've been using this place for years, the husband says,
hoping for a break, and Jimmy the sales guy starts double-talking
deals so dense they paralyze the cerebral cortex.
Yeah, a new car in hell, I'm thinking, fueled by dark matter,
serpent-salesman at the wheel. Get in, he snarls to a blob
of sinners flopped next to a steam machine.

The husband says She wants to trade in the Passat. The new one
doesn't need all the bells and whistles. Their little girl is zipping
around the showroom checking out the cars, calling out the colors.

I'm negotiating the best price on a Jetta, ducking the verbal net spun
of hunger and gamesmanship for six hours, and I'm starting to wonder
if this place is in fact a portal to hell.

I can't do anything about taxes, but I'll knock off the prep fee
Jimmy says, desperate to close the damn deal today. And wouldn't it
be right and good for me to buy this family the car?

Put them in it today, then walk out to the highway into the night, slip
the brace. And yet what are they to me, these charmed people who live
life as it unfolds, rather than observing it at the end of a stick.

My sales guy comes back with a figure. I'll sleep on it I say
and start to get up and he says What number would make you happy?
666 I'm thinking but I lowball him and he takes off again
to pretend to talk to his boss.

The girl shrieks, Dad, you could text on the screen, the seed of self sprouting.
I'm actually enjoying this, she says and the word *actually* is killing me
because it's a key to the kingdom of grown-ups.

I see the road unrolling. May she drive unharmed past the cyclopean malls, restaurants trawling for teeth, chain stores waving to her wounds. Drive on, girl, past all those who would snip the numinous buds that blink with joy.

Abridged

They are both the same,
innocent, defenseless as flowers.

When they are hurt,
they rush to each other
like blood to a bruise.

They buy a house and a car
and I am born.

When they wash me,
they see in my nakedness
the future blossom
into fountains.

If this were true,
I would not have
spent my life stooping
in perfect sunlight.

Blue

It's one of the things that happens

from the scattering of light.

It's similar to what makes a moon

blood orange or what makes us forget

we live in a straight line unless something,

a planetary life, gets in the way.

Light moves like a mirror or the flat face

of a prism as the sun goes down.

Blue light scatters and lets the reds and yellows

go right into our eyes. It's something

that happens before it gets dark.

Amor Fati

It's so hard to let go & get really scary
& say fuck whatever it was that fucked me,
but I am going to say it now,
I'm going to peek out my cave window
& finally say that there is a great ugliness
on the way & I fear it & know it & begot it
with the help & blessings of something
that meant no harm, was just empty
as a birdless sky.
Nobody saying anything.
Somebody wearing their best clothes
gets buried or burned & that's the way
things get done around here.
This harmless thing
as empty as snow, this thing
came from something
that meant no harm
& the world meant nothing to it.
What if I could rush into its arms
& kiss its dummy lips & let it drag me
into the woods without a fight & still notice
how the leaves are not just trembling,
but trembling with exquisite agency.

Black Rattle

for Dr. Irwin Badin

Sometimes my voice
comes out of your mouth—
songs rush from the throats of weeds,
leaves fly back to trees,
and the moon peels back its skin
to show the sea
its great green heart.

I used to bring you souvenirs from hell—
wasted chances in a screaming jar,
hours, months, tangled in kelp,
envy curled in a shoe.

I shook my memory at you
like a black rattle
and would've sacrificed
a city for a kiss.

It was in your listening
that I heard my voice
for the first time.
It rolled across my tongue
like luminous beads
and the sound roused me
from my drowned bed.

Fata Morgana

Before this moment with its pitfalls and false notes,
there was that late 20th century light that set the standard
for beauty, at least for me, right there on that table in Nice
under the Cinzano umbrella, when time was just a melancholy construct,
not personal yet, and any number of futures waved like palms in a dream,
when the holy trinity, coffee cigarettes notebook, offered refuge, and evening
as far off as old age, that affliction that only happened to the unlucky.

The Essex Mill, Paterson

For Mark

We finally met at the Roma Club on Cianci Street
when Angelo was king of the espresso machine
and the soccer trophies stood like centurions
among the philodendra and, across the street,
the blue metallic door of the laundromat
looked soldered shut.

You lived around the corner, at the Mill,
the artists' housing, when we sat in your loft
among the piles of books and, out in the back,
the ruins of the Colt Mill and the Allied Textile Plant
amid the weeds and bricks and old boards with nails
so big we could see them from the third floor.

And scattered everywhere: curls of corroded metal,
rocks, branches and bottle shards, as if they'd been flung
to the ground by a petulant god trying to unbuild a world.

I had never looked into someone's eyes without seeing
a diminished self, but that night in the loft, the doorknobs
gold as the sun went down, we looked at each other beyond
the broken things.

And afterwards we walked up the hill to the Great Falls,
past the hydroelectric plant, its turbines twirling like prima
ballerinas and past the gorgeous concrete steps leading down
to the river. When we stood on the bridge and could see the Falls,
they rushed forth over the cliff as if the earth had just begun.

The Lucky Daughter

In memory of my mother

The ivory figure of a Japanese peddler
saddled head to toe with baskets, masks,
and brooms was the most expensive thing
she ever bought with her own money.
I never wondered what he meant to her
with his eyes that seemed to be looking
through water and that smile that might've
been holding back a laugh at the grand
she spent on him.

Maybe she could read benevolence into him,
the father who would've applauded,
not beaten her, for the nudes she sketched
on her bedroom walls.

Maybe at dinner the peddler would tell
funny stories about his customers
and smile at her, the lucky daughter,
and each day would end like this,
not with her father's stories
of the dental lab, the flawless teeth,
his partner's thoughtless suicide,
this one's stupidity, that one's sloppiness.

Maybe she brought the peddler out of the land
of the inanimate so he would lead her out
of the land of the unloved to tell her
that she had always been good enough—
the rest, a spell cast by a clumsy ancestor.

The Bristol Plaza Hotel, Wildwood

From the fifth floor balcony
of the Bristol Plaza Hotel,
I watch families on the boardwalk,
parents in flip-flops and tank tops,
kids on invisible leashes running
up and down the steps to the sand
in that delirium of summer when
memory and history have just begun

And what would it have been like to have
had children, to unpack bathing caps and board
games, cough syrup and calamine, to wrap
bologna sandwiches in waxed paper and buy
peaches from the produce truck parked on the street
between the hotel and the dunes

And look at us, how happy we were, positioning
the blanket as carefully as a communion cloth,
placing a sandal at each corner, the Atlantic
behind us, ready to roll, and the kids
running into the waves with joyful terror
and I, exalted by love, carry them aloft
out of the sea

And all around, from Pompton Lakes,
Far Rockaway and Parsippany, people
come with can-openers and band-aids
and stories of splinters and shark scares
and we smile and nod at the way life
is unfolding at the Jersey shore while
the kids stick shells and bottle caps
atop their castles and run caravans
to and from the sea to fetch water
for the moats and ponds

And when the sun gets low in the sky,
we pick up the sandwich wrappers,
sweatshirts, and checkers, shake out
the blanket, pack the towels and tubes,
and the kids say heartbroken farewells
to their new friends who are leaving
for Metuchen in the morning, then we trek
to the shower at the bottom of the bleached
cedar steps and wash the sand from our feet
as the sea behind us stops swirling

And when it's nearly dark and the moon,
up over the Ferris wheel, is almost too big
for the eye to bear, we go to the boardwalk
and take our place among the generations
and I hold the hands of my children
and lead them to the ring toss and skee ball
and to the mechanical claw that descends
in somnolence from the ceiling of the glass tank
to hover above the hill of trinkets
and the arthritic metal fingers open
and grab onto a rubber spider, a skull ring,
or a capsule containing a pink plastic seahorse
and the claw lifts the prize as if it were Venetian
glass and drops it down the chute into the frantic
hands of my children who plead for more tokens
while the life-size gypsy, turbaned and bejeweled,
watches in malice from her lacquered ticket booth

And I lift my kids up onto the carousel horses
where they sit enraptured by the leather reins
and the lunatic eye of the horse looking backwards
and I live to glimpse their faces and fluorescent hair
as they ride by rising and falling to the old-world organ
and I will not be dreaming this or thinking
the way I always think, in dark conjecture.

Serenity Room

1

There are five recliners in a circle
each with a spongy blanket.
The lights have been dimmed,
but an aide has left behind her walkie-talkie
and it sounds like it's ready to lift off.
My mother is in one recliner, I'm in another,
an easy way to spend time now that she's afraid
of the color red and distrusts windows
as if the glass weren't there and the fingers
of the dwarf palmetto would reach in
and pull her down into its dark center
and cut out the last cluster of syllables
huddled beneath her tongue.

2

I look over to see if she's sleeping
and her eyes are open as though she's
forgotten to close them. Maybe
she's on some dusky street where
half-drawn figures drift into shadow
and vaguely familiar sounds almost
blossom into meaning. Maybe she opens
a door and glimpses the Persian rug she
hasn't seen in 70 years. Or the candy dish
laden with halvah and dried fruit.
Maybe her aunts from Brooklyn are there
and clutch her to their mountainous breasts
where she could stay forever.

3

My mother tries to inch out of the recliner
and an aide intercedes with a cup of apple
juice which she examines closely for poison
and studies her hand as if it's screwed
to her wrist. Then she brings the cup
to her lips as if it's the last thing left
from the world when she was Shirley
and carried keys, lipstick, cash.
And I hope that the cold, sweet liquid
brings a moment's pleasure but how can
it be that it comes to this, that at the end
you get thrown in the ring for one more
brutal round without enough stamina
to put on your shoes or enough strength
to say Thank you or Go to hell.

Serenity Room: Doris

A resident yells at an aide who's eating
out of a container: Stop eating!!! You're
already a big load!!! And the head nurse
barks orders over the clatter of dishes
and the phony chirp of television voices
and Dotty wanders in right out of the forties,
pageboy, cinched-waist summer dress
and serious beige pocketbook, she's all ready
to go out with her niece Pam who's a stock
analyst and won't be coming this week,
and now everyone is yelling
at poor Charlie who has wet his pants
and keeps trying to explain something
about a guy named Galinsky, and a sobbing
woman puts her head on the table next
to a plate of mac and cheese

My mother's trying to nap in the adjacent room
but Doris who's ensconced in a pillow-fortified
recliner is singing My Country 'Tis of Thee
with the only sounds available to her and does
endless maddening versions including one
that sounds like a twisted Latin mass.

Maybe the repetition keeps her from falling
into herself which is what I'm trying not to do
but I've already dipped my toe into a darkness
like no other and now Doris is working
on the word hospital, I think, but can only do
the hos part and tries with all she's got to push
out the p and these attempts are punctuated
by crying which I'm praying is some kind
of vestigial sound or audible pause
because what if it's pure sorrow
that got lost trying to find
the way back to reason.

Mt. Carmel Retreat

The first night, at dinner, during introductions, I blurt out
I'm Jewish, and two elderly women at the next table
check me out like I'm Lilith, demon-slut, sworn enemy
of the missionary position. A guy at my table slips me
a copy of Dark Night of the Soul and tells me St. John
of the Cross was a Carmelite.

I meet with Father Rob the next day, and he's my kind of guy,
zenned-out, left of center, psychoanalytic, no ego glowing
under the chasuble. To listen he said is to make someone feel real,
and he warned us about commercials, how they drag you
into the future away from love which only happens in the present.

The hospice worker from Hackensack tells me to be careful when I
leave to go home because Satan likes to snatch you by your broken soul
just when you're on the verge of salvation. There is a huge crucifix over
my bed, which seems to be saying Forget it, we only take good people.
All weekend the sheet metal shower thunders judgment and the linoleum
delivers a screed against excess. I'm lost somewhere between breakfast
and eternity.

But after mass on Sunday, Marguerite smashes her toe against a door
and someone hands me a bag of ice. I get on my knees, hold it to her foot.
A dark pride rises in my chest. Sister Linda, outsider, accursed and absolved,
forever longing for the parents in the monogrammed robes, tree lights
twinkling like winks from heaven.

American Express

The news anchor, dressed for drinks,
is telling me to enjoy my weekend
and I'm telling her it's not *my* weekend
—and all the others, the way they follow
you your whole life and mark the made-up
occasions for which I never voted, like I
would've ever put up my hand for National
Filet Mignon Month or Boss's Day. The way
they send you cards for free birthday dinners,
coupons for hearing aids, hair transplantation
or removal, brochures on above-ground burial,
the way they miniaturize mystery so you won't
be too awe-struck to cough up your hard-earned
cash for designer bags or gourmet dog food.
And the way they appropriate disasters for your
viewing pleasure and bring you The Storm
of the Century or Tsunamis Shatter Celebrity
Holidays or the way they label you The Boomers,
The Xer's, The Millennials and herd you through life,
a toll at every turn, and one day you're in a bed
wired for sudden movement, on horse tranquilizers,
and, in a moment of clarity, you see how it's done,
how they manufacture reality, how they play you,
cradle to grave.

Eternal Recurrence

I'm reading the news to him, the story
about the young guy from Teaneck
who killed himself at the Garden State Mall
with an assault rifle and I'm going on about
the stores locking down and the girl in Macy's
who made eye contact with the guy
and my husband says he can't take it anymore,
could I please just stop talking and that's why
we got rid of the television and now he's going on
about eternal recurrence and Nietzsche
and his all time favorite, Schopenhauer,
and he's talking about squirrels acting
in the same old way, saying if you're
a squirrel, you'll always act like a squirrel
and I'm saying squirrels aren't people
and what about progress, civil rights,
women's rights, gay marriage,
and he says change is a thin veneer
over the eternal truth and just how sick
he is of the same things happening over
and over and I look up eternal recurrence
and find amor fati. Imagine not just accepting
your fate but loving it, being willing to relive it
eternally, even thanking it for what it broke in you,
for what it burned in front of you, for how it showed you
every day, in increasingly ironic and inventive ways
how things might've been different.

It's So Odd to Accept the Terms of the World

1

That guy who had a fight with his wife
and downed three shots of tequila swerves
on Route 80 and all bets are off. A raccoon
chews through a wire in your attic and ignites
a carton of Christmas lights. Some cells go rogue
while you're buying the gouda and grapes.
You're operational at the whim of something outside
your range of vision that feels like physics with the whiff
of the sadist about it.

2

You got your start one day in prehistory
on the banks of a river when memory was just
a warning system, when two early humans
had insect-crushing, lousy sex that set into motion
a wheel of genetic fortune that lands you in a hospital,
born into a room of giants, two of whom name you
and take you home. Your fate is encrypted inside theirs.

3

It's so odd to accept the terms of the world, to not spend
every second trembling, offering, begging. Instead, you live
among trees, your life-long companions. The sky hides
an endlessness the mind can't abide, but a silver ladder
curving down into an empty pool feels like faith.
And gladly you endure doubt and the knowledge
of something always beginning to move out
of the shadows.

Change of Plans

Beneath the stockrooms, in the vengeful dirt,
weeds and roots mobilize; shoppers mount
the escalators, thinking with their tongues;
a herd of electronic animals haul children
across the bling-blown concourse.

Me, I'm heading back to the cave,
stumping along in my stone shoes,
under a sky of pissed-off birds,
past rocks plopped in the dirt like refusals,
past mutant life forms living it up in the landfills.
I hear the furnace-born brains cranking out bad ideas
like bullets.

I'm sorry. I wanted to write something beautiful,
maybe a prayer of gratitude for weight-bearing bones
or an elegy for ice.

Walt Whitman at Willowbrook Mall

I am the man, I suffer'd, I was there.
      —from Song of Myself

And all that is in Macy's is in me.
The fragrance I breathe is the fragrance
you breathe and I am happy here among
the throngs who carry keepsakes of the world
in sacks on their backs and speak into the air.
In the nail salon the fumes intoxicate me
and reek of the sweat of stars. I loaf in this
poem and know it is enough to be, to breathe,
to see the great racks of costume jewelry,
to handle the gloves and hats, to accessorize.
O I have as good as made the body-shapers,
shoes, and bedspreads. I have sat on benches
and in flights of reverie returned to the Body Shop
to celebrate myself among the moisturizers and soaps.
And in my reverie, I am scrubbed with seaweed and honey.
At the food court I hear the popping grease, the rush
of carbonation. I smell the won tons, the mammoth pretzels,
the pizza. These things are as much of me as the dust of the stars
though I miss the willows and the brooks and the absence of useless thing

Gear

These are the tweezers I use to pick
the burrs off my thoughts.

Here is the sack of inflatable hills I lug
from dream to dream.

This is a fog machine clamped to my wrist
in case the dead come looking for me.

Here is the portable cave I roll through the streets
so I can bolt inside when right angles start to blur.

This is the stepstool I strap to my back
so I can look at what happens next.

And these shoes, tattooed on my feet in utero,
compel me to go in the wrong direction.

I wear these bells so I know where I am.

Still Life with Concealed Cave

I want this painting to go away. Leave the blue-lavender grapes,
eleven of them—or are they ovaries?

The pear looks as if it were cut with a guillotine—or are the halves
anatomical models of a uterus?

And what's that thing that looks like a bedpan or tricorne hat—
or prosthetic mound of Venus?

But the thing is, a story is coming against my will: Diego's vast
supply of sperm, Frida's crippled uterus, the barbarous burden

of the human body, the torments of the meaning-making mind. Is it too late
to retract the things I saw? To untell the story? If only I could see

the world unrepresented, the seals sunning on the rocks of Málaga before
they become cave art.

Birds

When a bunch of us were crammed into an office smoking,
you said I'm going home to let my birds out of the cage
and I said Mike, do you mean that metaphorically? And everyone
laughed, including the department chair, and I was so cool in that
moment, but I caught the nanosecond of dismay on your face,
which answered my question: No, I really do need to let out the birds
that were born inside me, that peck at me day and night and there's only
one way they get out.

For what it's worth, I wish I hadn't said that.

Something Luminous

In memory of Mike Reardon

Someone found you dead
lying in a stream
under a footbridge
in Mt. Arlington, New Jersey
in the middle of spring—
maybe you tried, like Li Po,
to embrace the reflection
of the moon and fell in.

Maybe your eyes opened under water
and saw something luminous dart away,
provoking a moment of clarity so huge,
so unbearable, it is sent from your body
and forms a cloud the size of everything
that went wrong, then disappears in the sky.

Not the bottle, not brains, not anything
could stop the slow moving tornado
formed at your birth from sucking you into
its gray mouth and spitting you out under the bridge,
a sharp rock your last pillow.

Nothing Is Altered but the Past

What was a girl in a white dress
becomes a figure in white

what was the ding of a doorbell
becomes the prophesy of the bell

a blistering kiss becomes the collision
of two souls.

No rain waiting to fall in late afternoon
or shafts of light trying to look eternal

no luggage leaning against gleaming footrails
as strangers raise a glass in amnesic hope

or missed flight that changes everything. No glorious night
outside of time in tangled sheets, moonlight resurrecting

dried hydrangea on the dresser, and there is no childhood illness
confining you to bed, where your gift is revealed in due course.

There is just this drifting that is always moving away from, never towards.

Hypothesis

The light ignites

the clouds

that gather over the river

like the thoughts

of the river &

into the minds

of the birds that rise

from the reeds

the way we rise

surfacing

without consent

from our dreams.

To know nothing

must be a tribute

to something—

or a dereliction—

or holiness itself.

Like a Lotus

Weeds, grass, wild onion, their light once entered my eyes
for the first time. Once I tasted dirt and it was good: the pebbles,
a revelation and warning. The future fallout of our lives together
collected in conduits under the floors. A cell in the attic held
our violent twins. If only I could shake off the coat I was born in.

Instead I buy something that makes less of me, as if this thing
could leach away my envy or snatch me back from the vanishing
point. Before the crib-side curses kicked in, there were lovers,
mysterious cheeses and fruits, landscapes that permanently
alter the eyes.

Still, I act as if my life will open like a lotus. And so what if things didn't
turn out the way I dreamed them. Other things happened. But not as good.

Memorious

There's the guy from the Borges story, Funes, who fell
off a horse and could suddenly remember everything:
the eye of a squid, the shadow of a shoe, each groove
on a peach pit, an intensity of detail so relentless that
to unwind he would picture himself at the bottom
of a river being rocked and destroyed by the current.
Equally odd is to have forgotten most of the days you
once inhabited, each with its own clouds, stones, water,
words said out loud. It's like living in a city where streets
are removed while you sleep.

Ancient Peoples

The gods roll the sun into the sky,
dump the fish in the rivers,
inflate the clouds, hand-operate
the animals and finally settle
on who gets a bombshell
and who gets a breather.

Down below, newlyweds stroll
the fruit stalls and buy a pomegranate,
hoping the wet seeds ignite a pregnancy.

A man is cleaning clay
from his nails with a broken
reed and a woman is praying
to every known and unknown god
for the absolution of sins
she's not sure she committed.

No one is thinking about
their bowls and beads
or that receipt for three goats
ending up under glass.

Or how someone from the future
will imagine that boy tossing
a melon down the steps,
the shadow of a fern
on mud brick eclipsed
by the sudden swing
of his mother's hand.

Palace Cake

Mud is big here.
You can hear the suck and swish of it
as a woman scoops it into a bowl.
She isn't thinking Hey, look at me
over here, living in the Ancient World.

The fish-jammed rivers flash silver.
Folks wolf down barley cakes and dates,
kids play with their tiny clay animals,
a couple eats fried fish to die for in Nippur.
And everyone dreams of sinking their teeth
into a piece of palace cake.

An elder is foretelling a disaster. The listeners
lift an arm in prayer, hearts tight with terror, any
minute a ticked off god could kill a crop, send
a flood, or take a kid.

Some folks throw stones at a woman who
had snagged two husbands. Her crime
is inscribed on each stone. As she loses
consciousness, she thinks neither one
was worth a fig.

Despite the jaw-dropping inventions, gorgeous
jewelry and nature still pristine, Sumerians live
in a world of hurt. Look at the big sweet shocked
eyes of their figurines.

And we'd be anxious, too, if we only had a couple
of rosettes and a few agate beads to protect us
from a host of pissed off gods who only made you
in the first place so you could wait on them—
just to end up in some muggy afterlife with a mob
of depressed ancestors.

No one wanted to become an ancient people
with their combs and bowls, wills and weapons
catalogued in distant lands where no one could see
their cuticles, chapped lips, sun-seared shoulders,
or feel the heat beneath their sheep skin skirts—
or see them trembling as they read the messages
in the comet-crazed sky.

The Philosopher

He's sitting there in the recliner, coffee in hand,
staring at the ghostly place on the rug in front of me
where the ground-in food has created a permanent
stain we call *The Shroud of Turnip* and I say
What zone are you in today?

And he says Socrates Zone and I say Look at you
thinking about Socrates Saturday morning
and he says Yeah, he's considered a sophist
and I go Tell me what that is again and he says
He uses words to bullshit someone into buying
his argument and I'm thinking What's wrong with that,
I do it everyday.

Philosophers don't like him anymore, he says.
Wittgenstein was the first guy to put the kibosh
on him. The only reason Socrates gets any air
time is because you have to go through him
to get to Plato.

And now he's saying that Wittgenstein said
we shouldn't be asking the same questions
if they haven't been answered in 2,000 years

Amen to that I say…

But I'm thinking how laid back and cool
Socrates was, the way he blew off the state
and threw back the hemlock like a shot
of Sambuca.

But what do I know about philosophers
except for my husband who loves living
in a cloud inside a giant snow globe
in a universe in which I may or may not exist.

The Armenian Home

My mother has begun to snore
and the sound is terrible, like she
has a clam stuck in her throat.
She's lying there wearing
the pink sweat pants I got her
at K-Mart and the flowered top,
courtesy of the laundry ladies
who bring her clothes from
the newly-dead.

Outside the room, up and down
the cocoon-colored halls, the alarms
are ringing like the bells of hell
and I can see the black wheelchairs
parked in front of the nurses' station
like metal spiders clutching
their prey.

On the television that never turns off
a commercial for Abilify is saying
how in elderly dementia patients
this drug may cause death as if
death weren't already being caused.

The music director is singing next door
and turning By the Light of the Silvery Moon
into a killing machine. I'm praying she doesn't
come in here, though, if she does, maybe I'll
grab her by the throat and squeeze the last note
out of that godforsaken windpipe.

My mother's snoring has grown ambitious,
as if her lungs are two machines
trying to catapult her into another life.
Go back to your mother for a while, I'd tell her,
ditch the cold father, never get married, never
have children, move to the Village, have parties,
be a painter—dump the old life in the river
and watch it float away.

Son of Sam

The voice coming from next door
to give meaning & direction
to the dying hole inside, the .44
caliber exploding a kiss, blowing
the kicks, spit & epithets
to kingdom come & the voice
all the time telling you
this action must take place
for it will cure & restore
the diseased trees, the shrunken fruit,
the rodent heart; it will remove
the gray thing from the apartment
in Yonkers, steady the tilting sky,
stay the hand of the father in Florida
fixing the ceiling fan for the new wife
& it will purify & rectify the earth
in which your mother with her dirt-filled
womb resides & all you have to do is listen
to the neighbor's dog telling you exactly
what must be done to put things right.

Salt

We're driving across the George Washington Bridge
heading back to Jersey and a saltshaker appears
in his hand which is lying on his lap, his other hand
on the wheel, and I'm thinking Holy crap, did he
just pull a saltshaker out of his pants? And he starts
shaking it out the window and I go What are you doing?

And he says It's my mother and I say What? Then he says
You know, her ashes, and I say Shut up, you're scaring me
and he says C'mon, you know she loved the Hudson.

And now I'm covering my face against the blowback
and rolling up the window to stop the draw and trying
not to do one of those laugh-cry yelps, picturing the times
I saw her use a saltshaker at Sardi's or The Heidelberg or put
one on the table all those Friday nights in the Hackensack
apartment and I'm thinking that everything we say or do
has its own little future—and know for sure my own grim
irony is in play.

Now he's saying Yeah, I sprinkled her at the Met, too, and I go
Where, in the Lehman Collection? I'm flashing back to him acting
weird, not getting off the bench, staring straight ahead even as I
wave to him to come see Reclining Nude by Suzanne Valadon
and his feet doing something strange like they're moving on their own
and I say Why didn't you tell me you were gonna do this and he says
You woulda spooked me.

And then he says Yeah, I was lucky, the guard was zombied-out,
and now he's putting the shaker in his jacket pocket saying
I still have more, for the Delacorte maybe, but I'm gonna use
a parmesan shaker next time as he swings onto the Palisades Parkway
asking me what we need from Stop and Shop but his voice sounds like
it's being broadcast from a root cellar and I'm sitting there marveling
at the idea that he would risk arrest at a New York institution for a woman
who broke him like a wishbone.

At the Shore: End of August

Baptismal fog, fountains,
real and imagined, the sea
that paralyzes the mind

You lived inside your mother
you were released

Time was a leisurely construct,
flattering, generous, even kind,
before it flashed open like a knife

There were things to think about,
to do, to see—the world loves
to flower in flames before
it forgets you

The Royal Mineral Water Hospital, Bath

I checked into the Royal Mineral Water Hospital in Bath;
my feet were killing me, two enraged subjects
who'd rather beat you to death than obey

the sisters soaked them in seltzer every day
and talked to them about service, calling them
faithful servants

the doctors blamed the pain on comets and said
the affected bones would no longer be visible
in x-rays

when the chaplain confessed he was scared
of scapulars, the sisters rolled him up
in a blanket and stowed him in a mop closet

in the ward hung a painting, The World is His Footstool,
and I couldn't stop wondering how it would feel to be that
at home in the universe.

Bath

This is the city where
Queen Victoria, as a girl,
so the story goes,
alights from a carriage
into a wigged out crowd
when a wind whips up her skirts
revealing the royal nether garments
fluttering like lost souls

the crowd goes crazy
laughing and back-slapping
until the English sun shrinks
to a burning bean
and lodges in her throat
where it sticks
for the rest of her days

and henceforth and forever
her horsemen are ordered
to circumvent the city
that had loved her, truly,
if only for one glorious moment.

Calculations

We're waiting for our copying jobs
at Staples, so she starts chatting me up,
says she's a retired math teacher.
When I tell her I taught English,
she says that English teachers
are the worst and she always kept
her mouth shut at the book club
because they always wanted
evidence and she just wanted
to talk, have a cup of tea,
what's the big deal?
And I'm being too nice as usual
making it clear to her I'm not
one of those book bitches.

Now I'm hearing about the math museum
in New York and I can tell she wants someone
to go with. I'm brainstorming excuses
but it's my turn to say something so I say
how much I like zeros and that I even
tried to read a book about them.

Now she's telling me how she used to prove
to her students that she can get 2 to equal 1
and keeps saying Let A=B and it's like
God's saying it, but now she's saying Anything
can be anything and this is starting to sound
like patent bullshit and she's droning on
and I'm so glazed out I can only nod and say hmmm
like I'm Bertrand Russell finally grasping the true nature
of mathematics when all she wants is some tea and company
and it's her bad luck that it had to be me she ran into,
the Queen of Zero.

Witness

It's funny how natural it is
like I'd always seen her
bucking and shaking
and holding onto the safety rail
while an aide wipes her ass

It's no big thing now
the way her toenails
look like ancient teeth
and her hands like two
jellyfish bobbing
around her torso

Like her arms and legs
had never looked like
anything but purple tentacles
as if she were beginning
to turn inside out,
the skeleton pushing
aside muscle and artery

It's business as usual now
wheeling her to the dining room
as she tries to propel herself
from the chair with her last ounce
of strength, she is not going
gentle into that shitty night
and I'm proud of how she fires
off NO, her last line of defense

But when I walk in as the aide
is undressing her, her right
breast is a testament to all
that was given and to all that
was lost, and the scar tissue
on the left, a searing indictment
of a careless god.

Private Sales

Wherever you are, I hope you're fitted out
with a body, one you like, sturdy, sexy
and with clothes from Johanna's At-Home
Shop where you got the silk-lined army green
alpaca coat with the rhinestone clasp.

When you wore it, you looked like you were
off to catch a plane to Monaco or Madrid
where you'd be free of me, the crying
machine strapped to your knee, not off
to some steak joint or Mother's Day Brunch
at the Marriott.

Though you said no way you would've actually
taken the pill your father gave you, still, I always
wondered if maybe you did and it worked a little,
rendering me half-girl, half-ghost.

The Theory of Soul Mates

My husband's saying Ya know, Feynman thought
your past could be your future and now I'm listening,
my hair growing long and dark again, my bar stool
at the West End coming into view.

And now he's talking about QED and I say Isn't that
the shopping channel? And he says It stands for quantum
electrodynamics like everyone knows this and starts going on
about quantum this and quantum that when I hear a word
I recognize: lamb, but he's saying lamb shit and I say What?

Lamb shift he says and I'm seeing a lamb gently shifting gears
on a little tractor and he starts saying some gibberish about shifting
away from established theory.

I'm totally lost until he says that Willis Lamb won the Nobel Prize
in Physics in 1955 and for the hell of it I pull up his obit and find out
that he had three wives, one of whom was named Bruria, and I'm trying
to hear Willis saying her name in the sack—and wondering how the hell
he went back to sleep for two hours after Sweden called—and marveling
at how he died of gallstone complications after spending his life communing
with the invisible.

My husband's saying that if he could go back to the past he'd grow up
in Michigan, not New Jersey, and I say Yeah, but then we wouldn't have met
and he says But you wouldn't know I existed if you never met me.

And that doesn't bother you? I say. Hey, this is purely theoretical he says.
This isn't real. Yeah, exactly what I'm thinking.

With No Thought of Skull

If you are enamored of round things,
go to seminary or become a glass-blower

If you are certain of the skeleton within,
go be a builder of boats or a violinist

If it's silence you seek, be a baker
or tight-rope walker or deep sea diver

If you worship weather, become a storm chaser
so ardent that death is a bargain

Or if you're looking for simple faith,
cut hair with no thought of skull

I'm telling you, don't walk away like I did.

Invocation

Shadow of a Shadow, grant me

the ambition to search for hairpins

and finials in hotels along the sea,

to sleep on mattresses sanctified

by sweat, to behold pigeons

on a balustrade, who, in heroic,

genetic obedience, tic and cock

their lustrous heads. Illuminate,

with your rising eye, every waking-

sleeping moment: the bank clock,

the dolphins guarding the fountains,

the boy at his window, waiting

for wings.

Revision

Stand still right now. This is your chance.
Tell the guy with the ponytail you're taking off.
Put down the drink. Grab a cab and go home.
Don't stop at that bar on the Upper West Side.

Take off the Lucrezia Borgia rings, the Afghan bangles
and Balinese earrings. Shower off the Shalimar. Put on
the corny slipper socks that no man, except the super,
has ever seen. Don't call anyone. Don't read. Don't smoke.
And stay away from mirrors.

Soon you will hear a voice that sounds like a newborn
with a ten-word vocabulary. This will be your first attempt
to form an honest sentence. You'll grab your makeup kit
and get ready to hit the bars along Broadway, see who's there.

But stay put. You can do this. You'll be here in the morning,
still in your twenties, with a drop of truth on your tongue. Maybe
it'll be September, leaves sprinting in circles on the sidewalks,
trash cans standing like little kings in front of their brownstone castles.

And you'll get dressed like a girl in love with books, not flattery,
and you'll walk over to the Hungarian Pastry Shop across from St. John
the Divine and on the way all the windows on 110th Street will whip open
and everyone will wave and wish you luck, and you'll break into a run,
future remorse rising from your skin like steam from the city streets.

Nieves Penitentes

The snow is falling
as if it's forgotten to stop.
Maybe the mind
that keeps mountains
upright and oceans
in their bed
is setting up some new venture
and I wish I could begin again,
born in a bird's mouth
in the drunken forest,
into full being,
not some stick figure
stilting around an empty lot
scratching messages in ice.

The sky is gone and above
the snow, nothing.
The people I have loved
and hated, who gave me
the world and took it back,
are under the snow.
Their longing almost killed me.
And I see now how silent
my world always was.
I see the things I didn't
even know to wish for.